This book belongs to:

Taylor

Kera till

Dottie Polka's Vintage Collection

A sketch-doodle-drawing book
for would-be fashion designers

little bee books

For the projects in this book you will need:

Colored pencils or crayons

Pen or pencils

Paintbrushes

Eraser

MOD MODE

STYLE! BEAUTY!

Fashion magazines for inspiration and to cut out examples of things you like

Colored craft paper

Watercolor paints

Scissors

Glue

And anything else that inspires you.

Hi, I'm Dottie Polka.

Just between you and me, that's more of a pseudonym of mine. But nowadays even my friends and customers call me Dottie, as well as the mailman who refers to me as Miss Polka whenever he brings the mail.

In my shop I sell items which already have a history—clothes, handbags, and all sorts of accessories—and unique pieces you just won't find anywhere else.

Of course these have been previously owned and used, but I prefer the term "vintage."

Back in the day when traders were unsure about an item's origin, they would refer to it as vintage.

But don't think that my shop smells like old mothballs! Everything is clean and and in good shape, and occasionally spritzing a bit of perfume using my vintage perfume atomiser helps too!

Selling is never a problem for me, but finding new pieces is. To find worthy items, I have to travel a lot. My favorite hunting grounds are the flea markets of the world—not all of them of course.

Let me share my favorites with you: Puces in Clignancourt, the Bacon and Flea Market on the Chatou Islands, the annual market in Lille, the Auer Dult in Munich (held three times a year), London's Portobello Market, and El-Rastro in Madrid. And occasionally I travel even further to the "Thieves Market" of Tepito in Mexico City.

Dottie Polka.

Of course, when I'm traveling I can't be in my shop at the same time. So I put up a sign that reads "Out hunting for new pieces," which can make my customers a little bit impatient sometimes. But it's worth the wait because they know that I don't just bring back great vintage fashion finds, but also rare fabrics, cute accessories, and amazingly stylish shoes of course!

You can find all these amazing things in this book as I show you my wonderful vintage world. So let's go . . . at a Polka Pace!

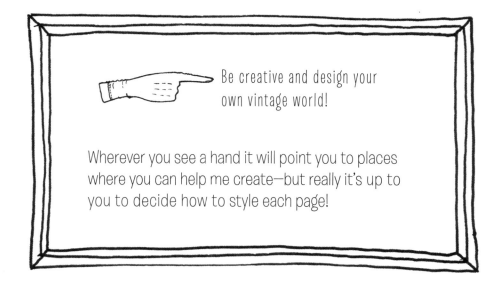

Be creative and design your own vintage world!

Wherever you see a hand it will point you to places where you can help me create—but really it's up to you to decide how to style each page!

polka dots

I still owe you an explanation about the meaning of
my name: "Polka dots" is the term used to describe
a dotted pattern in England and in America!

I hope you like the name as much as I do! It reminds
me of the confetti during a carnival, the blanket of
stars on a clear summer night, or fairy tales about
a girl showered in golden coins.

polka dots can be found on:

Clothes . . .

. . . shoes . . .

. . . furniture . . .

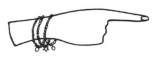 Where can you find polka dots? Draw them here or glue pictures of them on this page.

. . . and even tea pots.

 Play around with your favorite colors and create your very own polka dot design.

The designer Diane von Fürstenberg created the first wrap dress 40 years ago. Her dress has since become a fashion classic. It's even been exhibited in the Metropolitan Museum in New York.

Clutch bag

Wrap dress

 Decorate these clothes and accessories with polka dots. Try as many ways as you can think of: draw, paint, or stick them on. Be creative!

Pleated skirt

Knee-high socks

Coat

Smartphone cover

High heels

Handbag

T-shirt

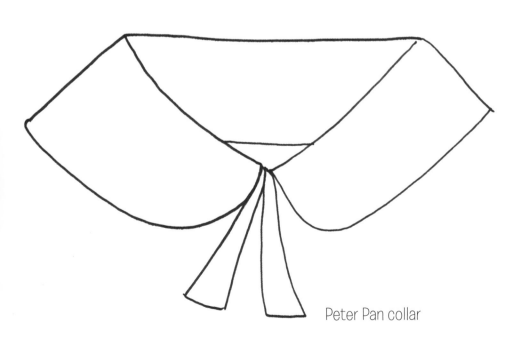

Peter Pan collar

Platform sandals

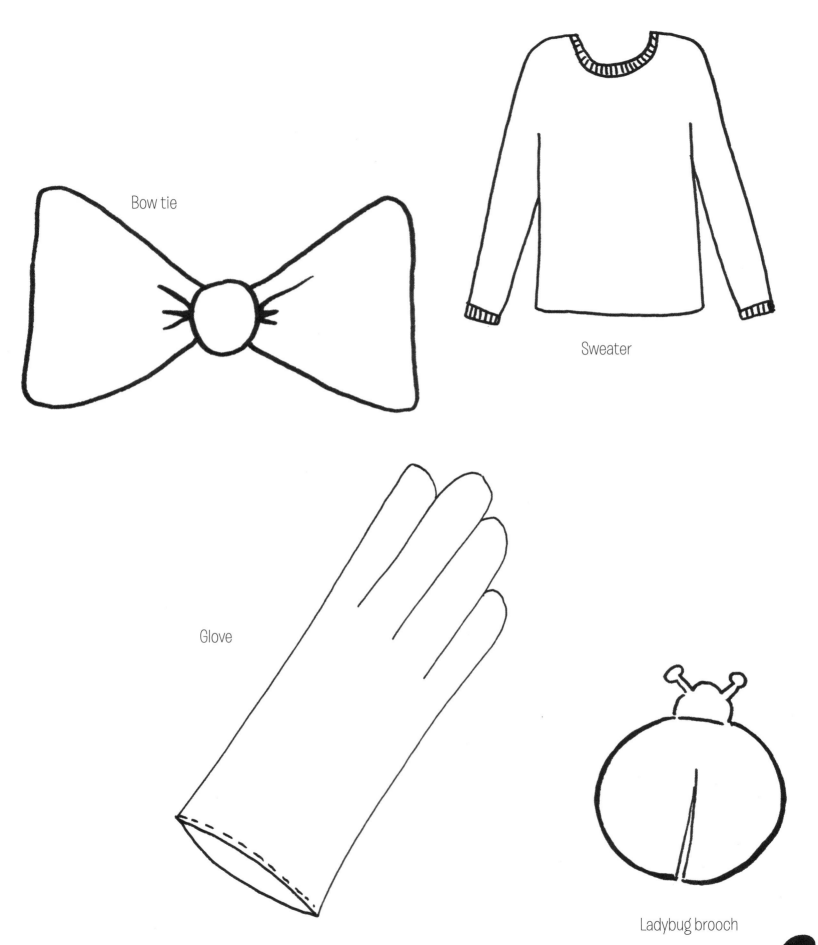

Bow tie

Sweater

Glove

Ladybug brooch

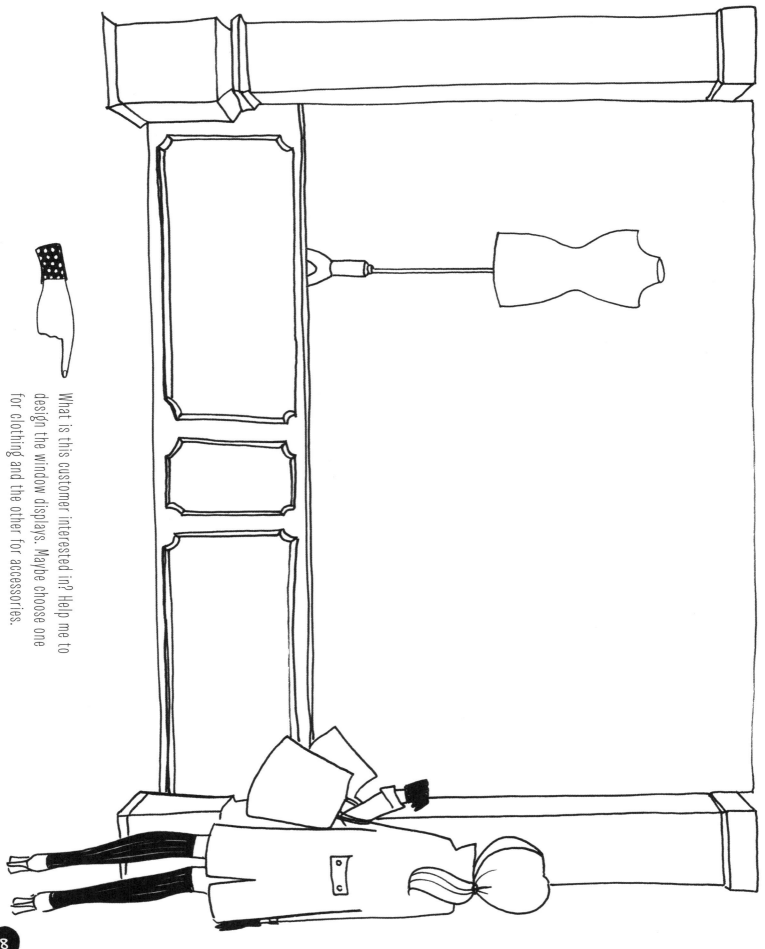

What is this customer interested in? Help me to design the window displays. Maybe choose one for clothing and the other for accessories.

In the 19th century, ready-to-wear clothes weren't easily available to buy. Women made everything themselves or arranged for a seamstress to visit them at home. The seamstresses were poor because they had to buy all the fabric themselves, and they would not be paid until the end of the year, if at all. Clothes became available to buy "off the rack" in 1870, thanks to the influence of the military, which made uniforms in regulated sizes. Clothing in standard sizes came onto the market at the same time.

Monsieur Boucicot was the first person to sell his clothes at fixed prices in his Parisian department store Le Bon Marché. Until then you had to ask for an object's price and then try to haggle it down!

My regular customers are allowed to haggle a little when they visit my shop. Otherwise I'd feel like I was selling my goods for too much!

price tags

Help me price my new finds. Use the price tags from the previous page and think about how much these items should cost.

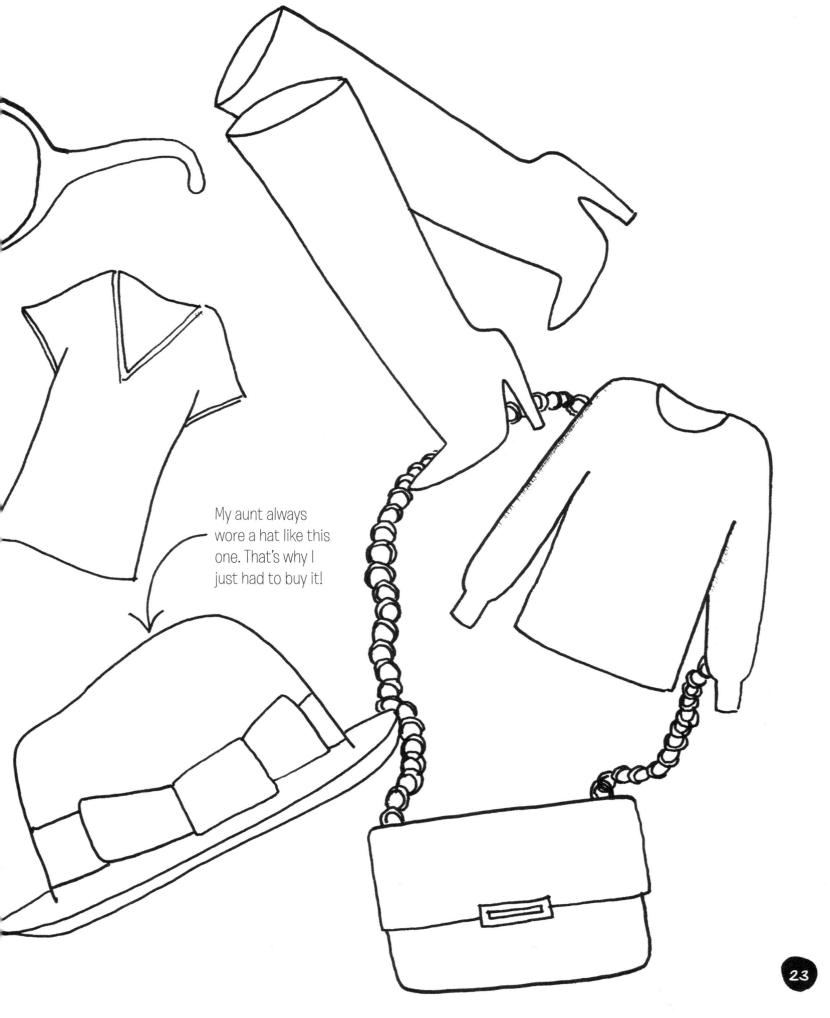

My aunt always wore a hat like this one. That's why I just had to buy it!

sunglasses

Sunglasses have been worn as more than just eye protection since the 1950s and have become a significant part of not only a woman's but also a man's image. Nowadays they are practically a status symbol.

Luxury, coolness, and freedom, as well as a measure of wealth, can all be reflected in a pair of sunglasses. Many famous clothing lines also have their own sunglasses lines. The right model is the icing on the cake!

 Whose sunglasses are these? Draw the face
behind them. How much do you think they cost?

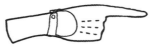 You can practice how to draw faces on this page. Try to think about what hairstyles might suit the sunglasses too!

 What face suits which sunglasses? Draw the best suited frames, or cut out ones you like from a magazine.

Some famous faces of the 20th century are difficult to imagine without their sunglasses!

· Greta Garbo
· Peggy Guggenheim
· Jackie Onassis
· Audrey Hepburn

Do you love little boxes and cartons as much as I do? My favorites are hat boxes that smell like lavender . . .

These bags contain beautiful bargains I found at a flea market. Tomorrow I'll take them to my shop.

Dottie's best pieces

This is where I collect and pin pictures of things my customers would like to find in my shop. Then I keep an eye out for them on my trips!

 What are your favorite pieces? Draw them here or use the wardrobe like a moodboard (see page 58) on which you can stick pictures, adding your own little descriptions.

Clothes hangers

My friend Daniel collects clothes hangers from the past. Most people back then used clothes hooks or pegs, but the clothes of the royal family, soldiers, and priests needed extra support for their hefty shoulder pieces and high collars.

Wooden hangers were used for these clothes, and you can still find them today. Later on, wire hangers were introduced because they were lighter and cheaper to produce. Nowadays you're given these when you get your clothes back from the dry cleaner.

I love old wooden hangers that have the names of the large fashion labels which no longer exist engraved on them.

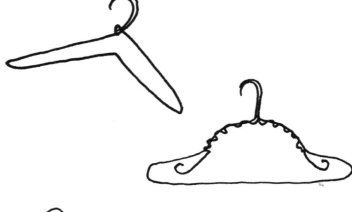

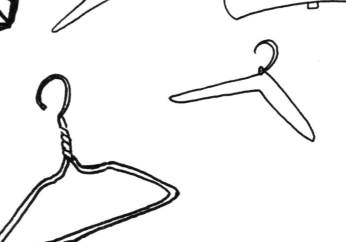

34

 Try to draw as many different hangers as you can without your pen or pencil leaving the page.

Close your eyes and draw some more clothes hangers.
How many can you fit onto this page?

Buttons in the pattern book*

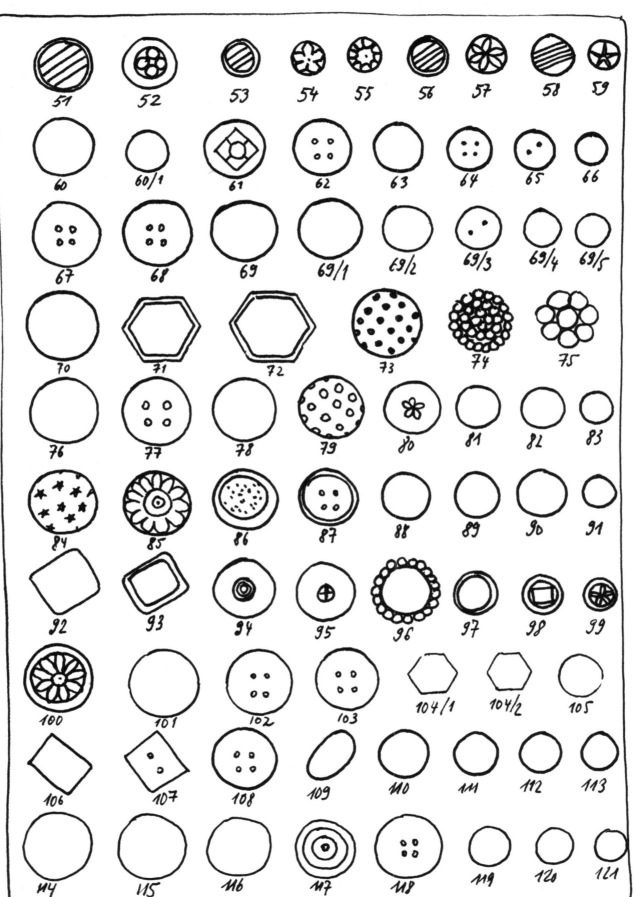

*Find out more about pattern books on page 179.

Draw in your favorite buttons or examples of buttons that you have found in the right spot below. You can also design your own beautiful buttons!

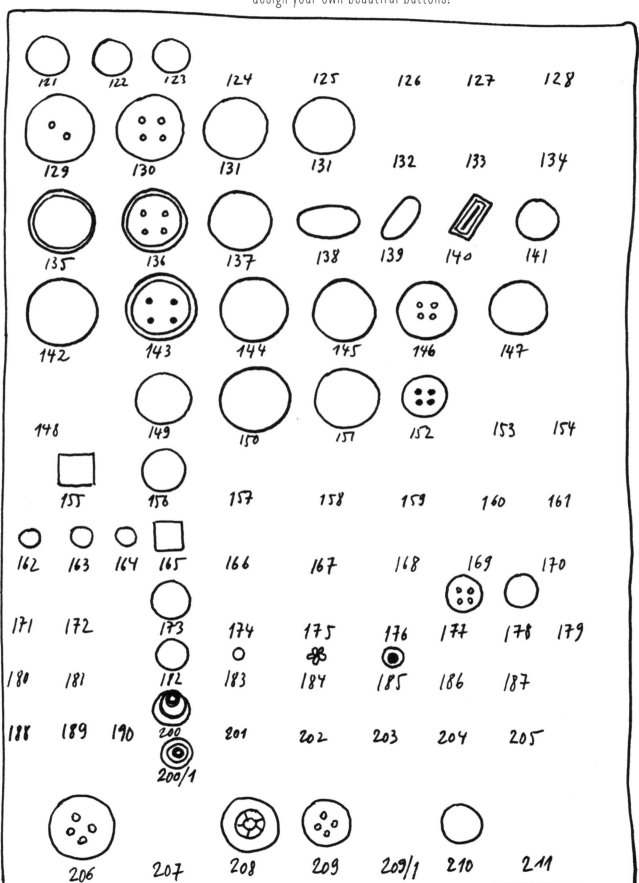

Cardigan

A cardigan isn't quite right without some buttons. Which buttons match these cardigans best in your opinion? Draw them on.

My grandfather always talked about the "cozy house jacket" he liked to wear on his days off. My grandmother had knitted it for him and he preferred it to a sweater, which he would pull over his head with a great deal of grumbling.

A better way to describe a house jacket is to call it a cardigan, which is the same thing of course. The term was coined by the Earl of Cardigan, who wanted to keep his soldiers warm in the biting cold of Russia with this item of clothing.

You can never have enough shoes!

You can find my latest shoe-bargains for my customers on these shelves. Which ones would you buy?

Some very famous women are renowned for owning more pairs of shoes than they could ever possibly wear. The French queen Marie Antoinette would change hers several times a day, and Imelda Marcos, former first lady of the Philippines, owned more than 5,000 pairs!

Nowadays, fashion experts still say that you shouldn't skimp on shoes. You can wear an old pair of jeans and a faded T-shirt, but your shoes should always be top-notch.

Maybe that's why women always line up at Christian Louboutin, the most expensive shoemaker in Paris. His creations are easy to recognize by their dark-red sole.

 Fill these shelves with shoes. They can be shoes you already own or ones you simply must have.

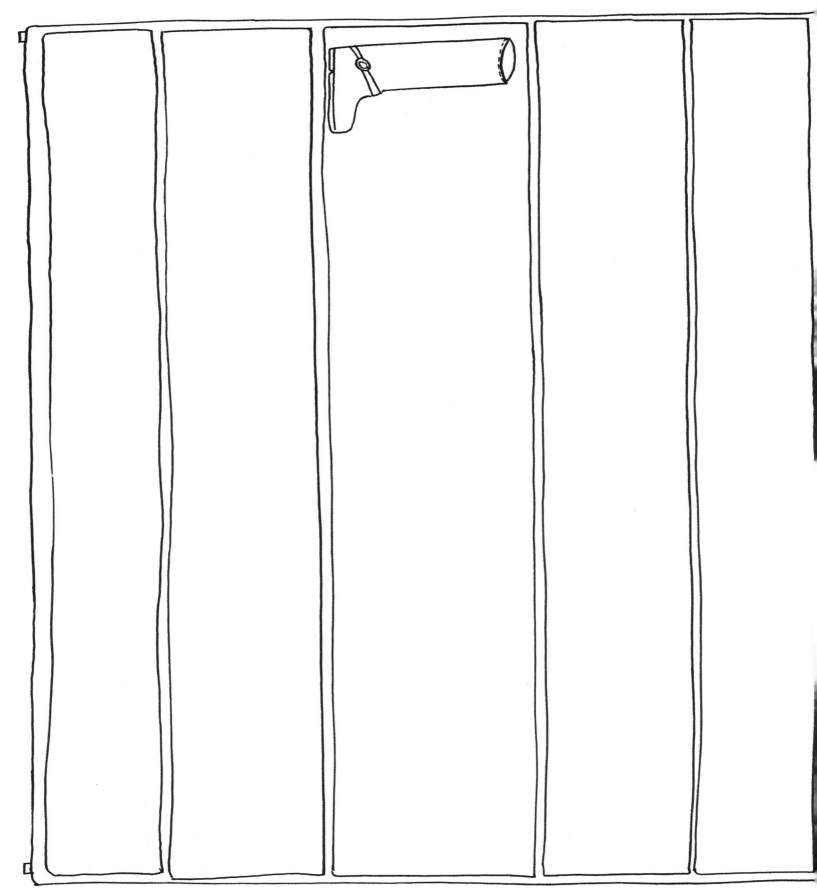

Draw, paint, or stick in pictures of shoes!

Booties   Riding boots   Flip-flops   Platforms   Ankle boots

Platform pumps

High-heeled sandals

Slingbacks

Boots

So many styles of shoes! Do you know what they're called? Try to match the names to the pictures.

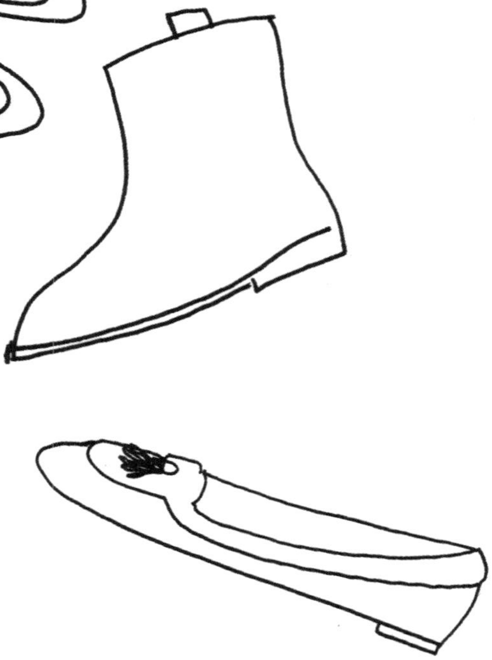

Slipper loafers   Peep-toe sandals   Tassel loafers

High heels Sandals Desert boots Chelsea boots

Heeled boots

Brogues

Sneakers

Ballet flats

Stilettos

Deck shoes Platform sandals Clogs

47

Draw the highest platform heel in the world!

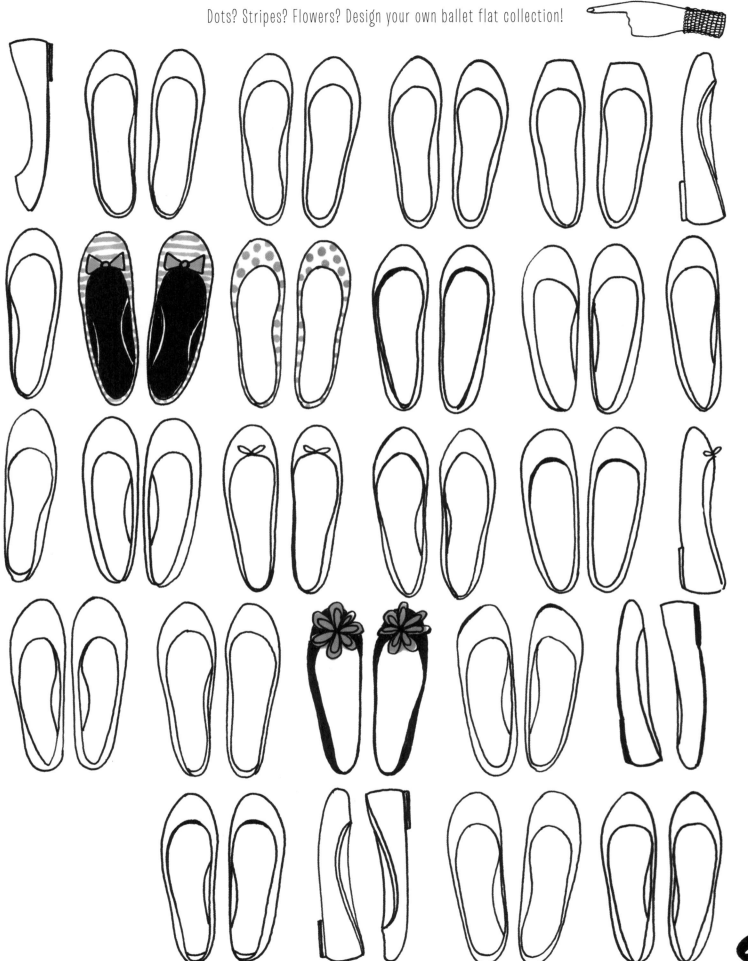

49

During the Ice Age, people tied rags of leather,
fur, or fabric around their feet as protection from the cold,
sharp stones, and thorny vegetation. From that simple idea
many different styles developed over time, including the
leather sandal—worn by Mediterranean people—or the
boots worn by the nomadic tribes of Central Asia.

Shoes often revealed quite a lot about the wearer's origins
and his or her position in society. Usually comfort was not the
priority; otherwise the stiletto heel, which you can see on this
page, would never have been invented!

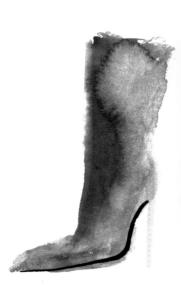

 Which heel do you like best?
Create more styles with them.

Dottie's travels

Every year I like to travel to different countries and cities to discover new vintage fashion finds for my customers. Sometimes I like to go to London for the weekend, and for the amazing flea markets in Paris I like to stay for at least a week. Or I spend three weeks exploring amazing bazaars and markets in Africa or Mexico.

What might I need for a weekend in London? Help me pack!

I wouldn't go traveling without this hat, not even for a single day!

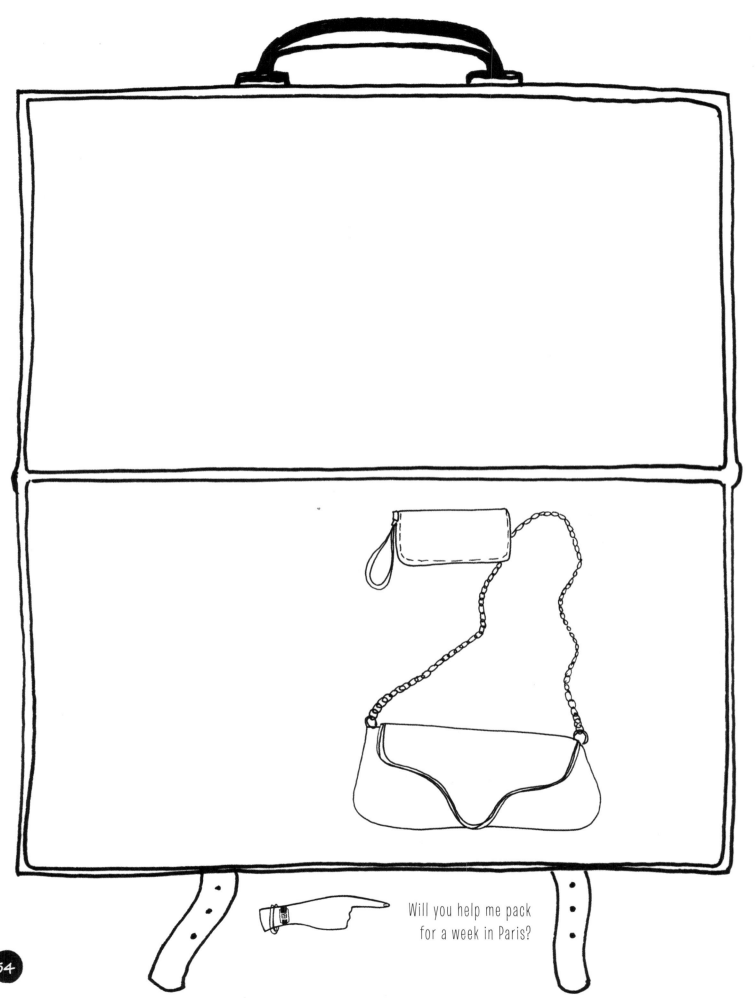

Will you help me pack
for a week in Paris?

Three weeks in Africa, I'm so excited!
What should I make sure not to forget?

55

 Isn't this rug lovely? I found it in a souk in Morocco.
Why not decorate it with a colorful pattern?

We come across patterns wherever we go, in repeating leaf patterns or a field full of poppies. What's your favorite pattern? Draw or paint it on this page.

Moodboard

A moodboard can be a large piece of
cardboard or a digital pinboard on which
photos, sketches, patterns, and any
written notes can be displayed or pinned.
You can express a certain mood on it, like
the colors for a new season in fashion.
I always create a moodboard after one
of my trips to create an impression of
the countries I visited.

Create a moodboard about a specific subject—maybe
for a new pattern for a wall in your room . . . or fun
fabric ideas for a new dress! Cut out pictures from
your favorite magazine, make sketches of things you
like, or print photos that you have taken. Simply collect
everything that fits your theme on these pages.

Draw the Mexican pattern from the previous page onto the top of this dress.

The unpronounceable quexquemetl is a sleeveless blouse, usually decorated with flowers or bird patterns. It is worn by the native women of Guatemala and Mexico. The famous artist Frida Kahlo loved to wear it and often painted herself sporting one as a sign of her Mexican heritage.

Quexquemetl

Kanga

Symbol

Border

Motto

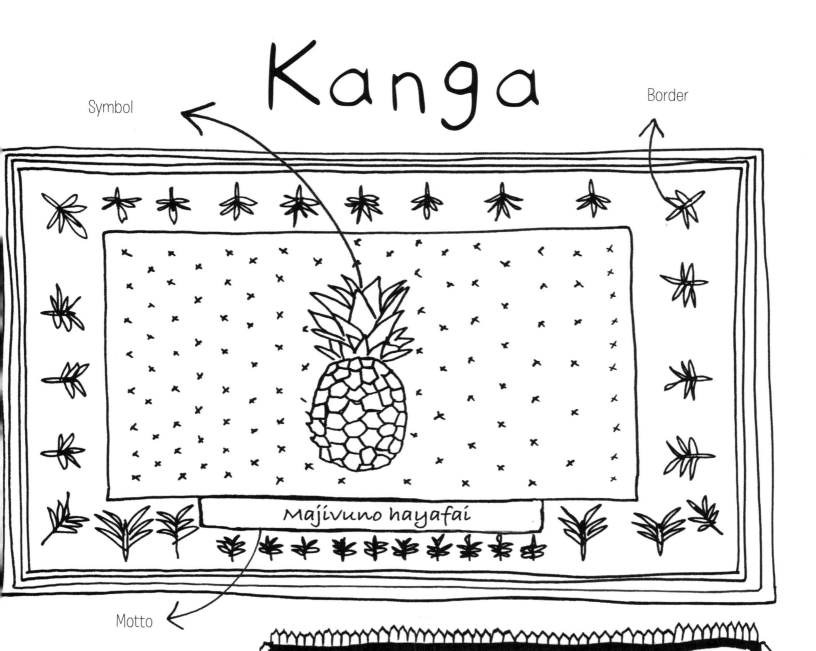

Majivuno hayafai

The women of central and east Africa wrap this colorfully printed cloth around their hips. A kanga is rectangular, measuring about 3-5 feet, with a wide border and a motto or image in the middle.

This one is inexpensive, yet a kanga can be funny and expressive, like a printed slogan on a T-shirt or sweatshirt.

"Kanga" is a Kiswahili word, and the motto is often in that language too. "Majivuno hayafai," for example, means something like "Greed isn't cool."

 Draw your own kanga. You can put your favorite fruit in the middle alongside your own motto.

I also sell dirndls in my shop. The most popular color combinations last year were red and blue. I wonder what it will be this year?

Kimono

No matter if it's a dirndl or a kimono, every national costume plays with patterns and colors. Try it!

Japanese fabric samples

portobello Market

Portobello Market crosses through London's famous Notting Hill area. Since the 1960s this has been the place for fresh fruit and vegetables, but on Saturdays you can also find second-hand clothes.

I once found some fantastic shirts for my boyfriend there, new but without the tags on. They had been skilfully removed. Only later did I find out that these had probably "fallen off the back of a truck." In order to conceal this, the thieves had removed any trace of the original owner and manufacturer.

 London is often rainy and gray. Give my coat some color!

Trench coat

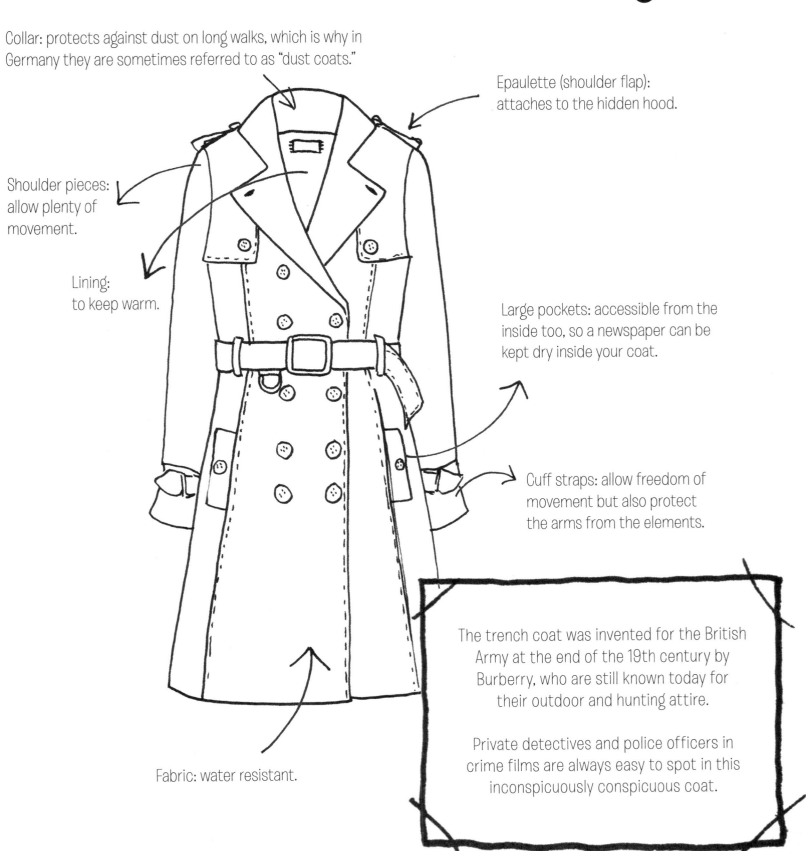

Collar: protects against dust on long walks, which is why in Germany they are sometimes referred to as "dust coats."

Epaulette (shoulder flap): attaches to the hidden hood.

Shoulder pieces: allow plenty of movement.

Lining: to keep warm.

Large pockets: accessible from the inside too, so a newspaper can be kept dry inside your coat.

Cuff straps: allow freedom of movement but also protect the arms from the elements.

Fabric: water resistant.

The trench coat was invented for the British Army at the end of the 19th century by Burberry, who are still known today for their outdoor and hunting attire.

Private detectives and police officers in crime films are always easy to spot in this inconspicuously conspicuous coat.

 The beige-colored military trench coat could use some color.
Use some neon to brighten it up.

Can you find celebrities or characters wearing trench coats?
Collect some pictures and stick them on this page, adding their names too.

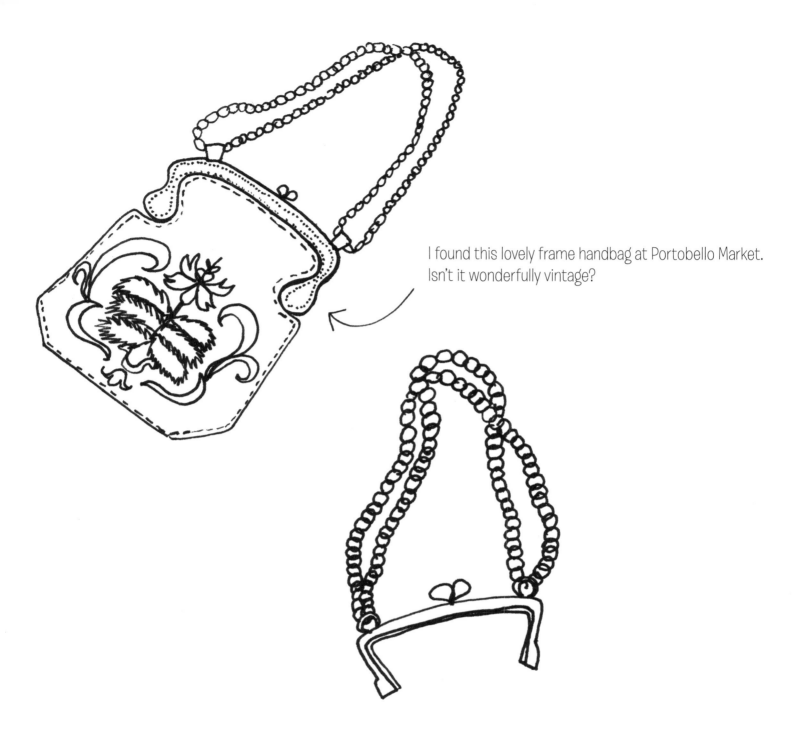

I found this lovely frame handbag at Portobello Market.
Isn't it wonderfully vintage?

 Design bags to match these clasps.

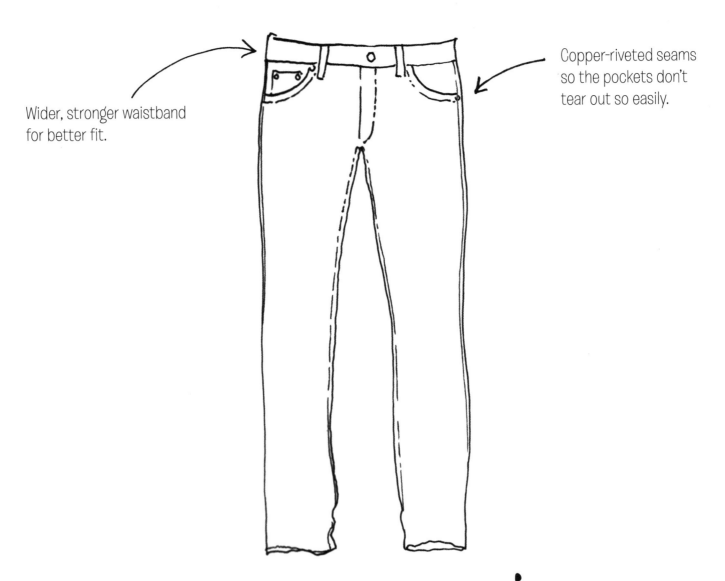

Wider, stronger waistband for better fit.

Copper-riveted seams so the pockets don't tear out so easily.

San Francisco

Jeans were first made for the gold miners in California.
The most important elements are still the rough sail canvas material,
the indigo blue, and the copper rivets which support and strengthen
the pockets. A vintage pair of jeans from 1880 earned its owner
$50,000 at an auction a few years ago.

The inventor of jeans, Levi Strauss, came from a town called Buttenheim
in Bavaria, Germany. The house where he was born is now a museum,
and his company, Levi's, still makes jeans to this day.

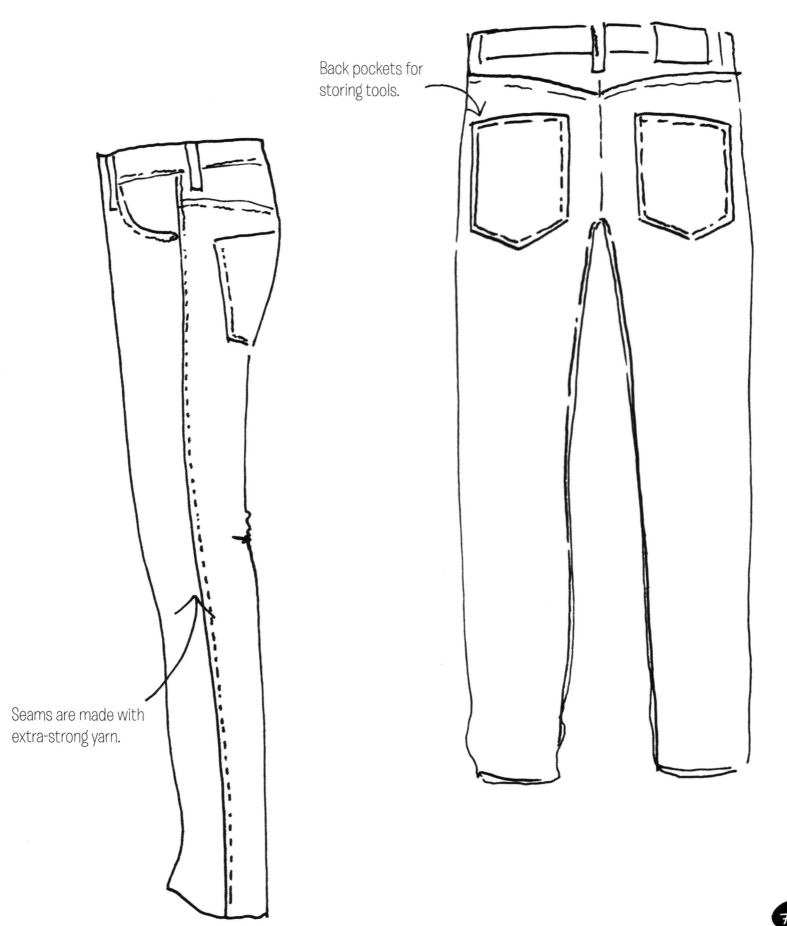

Back pockets for storing tools.

Seams are made with extra-strong yarn.

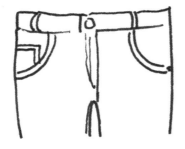

 Which is your favorite style of jeans? Skinny, boot-cut, or flared?
Draw the different types here.

"I wish I had invented blue jeans."

Yves Saint Laurent,
fashion designer

 For a while, jeans with patches were very popular because they used to look like worker's trousers. What other accessories can you think of? Decorate these pairs as much as you want!

T-shirt

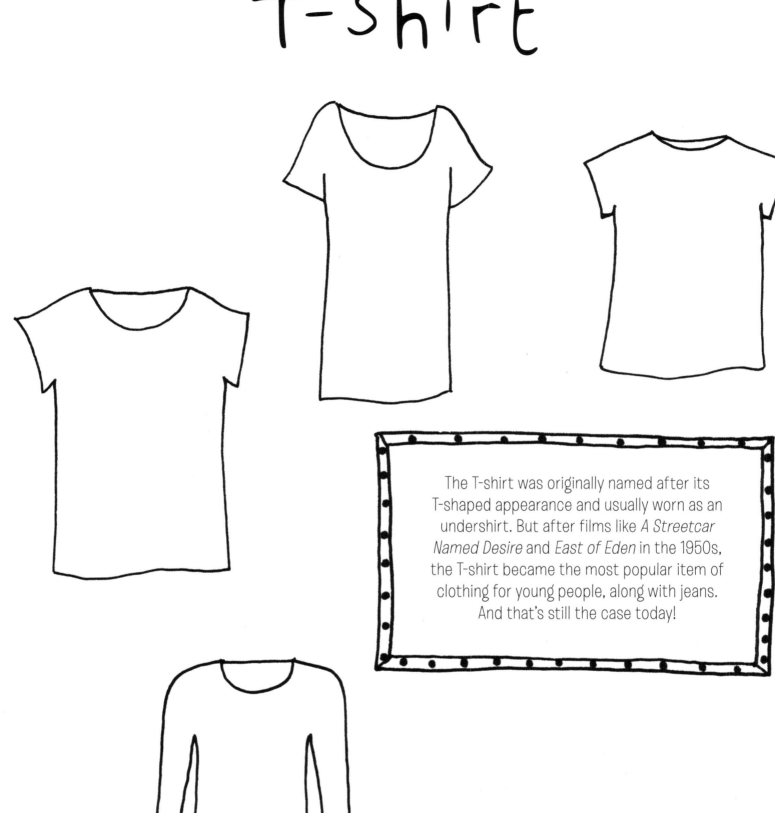

The T-shirt was originally named after its T-shaped appearance and usually worn as an undershirt. But after films like *A Streetcar Named Desire* and *East of Eden* in the 1950s, the T-shirt became the most popular item of clothing for young people, along with jeans. And that's still the case today!

Here you can see different styles of T-shirts. Decorate them with patterns, colors, and accessories, or even decorative holes. Then design your own shapes!

This T-shirt style is the one my customers like best.

paris

Accessorize this necklace with pearls. Be understated
or opulent—however how you like it.

Coral collier made from coral and gold, 1830
Musée des Arts décoratifs, Paris

Whenever I'm in Paris, a trip to the Musée des Arts décoratifs is a must. It houses priceless jewelry from long ago.

In the past you would wear a collier necklace with an evening dress for special occasions. Nowadays you can combine a collier, which is made of pearls, coral, or diamonds and precious metals, with a T-shirt.

Charm bracelet

A girlfriend of mine brought me back this charm from India. Can you guess where the others are from?

"A lot helps a lot" is an old saying that's certainly true when it comes to good luck charms worn on a chainlink bracelet. There really is no end to the number of symbols and charms you can buy: silver piglets, dice, tiny chimney sweeps, hearts from Tiffany's . . . The term "charm" probably refers to the idea that you have to charm someone into giving you one.

The tradition of wearing good luck charms has been around for a long time. Hunters in the Alps, for example, would carry a "charivari": a silver necklace worn on the waistband of their trousers that was said to bring luck on the hunt. The charivari would be passed down from father to son.

These old heirlooms are rare and very popular among collectors.

Design your own charm bracelet. You can find some charms to use on page 94, or think up your own creations.

 This is how I like to keep my favorite items of jewelry.
Would you like to add yours by drawing them in?

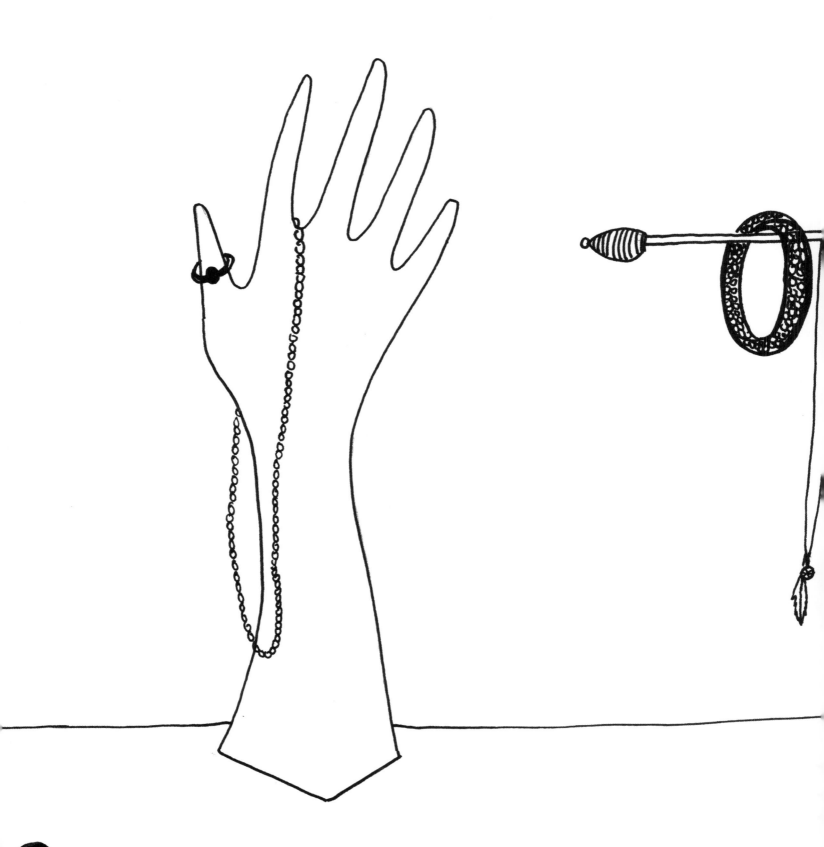

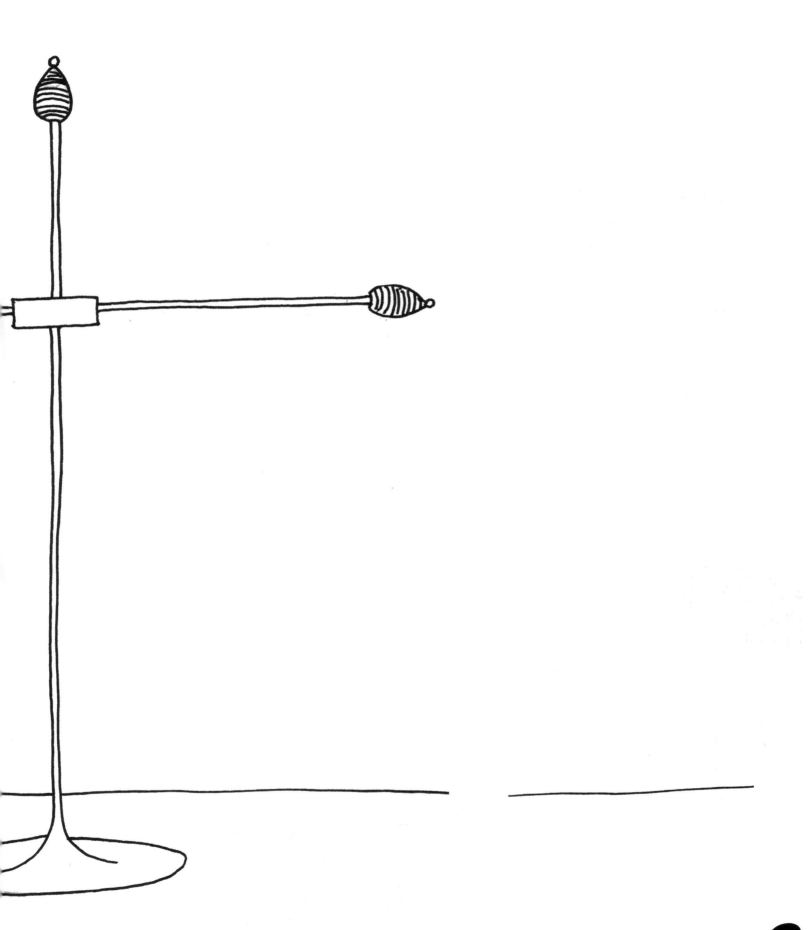

Earrings

I inherited this pair from my grandmother.

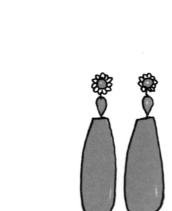

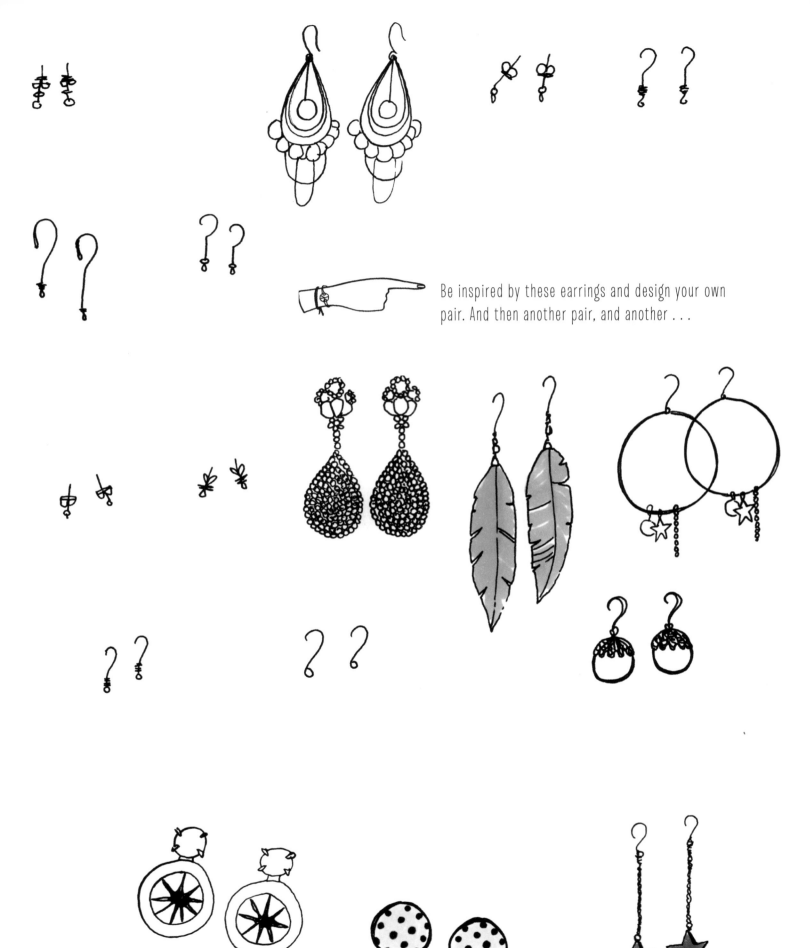

Be inspired by these earrings and design your own pair. And then another pair, and another . . .

Design some earrings for my customers. You can draw them, paint them, or create a collage from images in magazines.

88

Letter boxes

Letter or shadow boxes were traditionally used by printers to store the individual letters for the metal type that was used to print books. Letters such as "e" would appear more often in a segment of text, so they would be kept in the larger compartments. Rare letters such as "x" and "y" would be kept in the smaller ones.

As new printing methods took over from the traditional metal types, letter boxes were no longer needed, so they often ended up at flea markets. Many found their way to collectors who would keep small souvenirs and even specially made miniature objects in them.

There are many replicas, but an authentic letter box is easy to spot because of the little scrapes inside, as well as by the size and arrangement of the compartments. These are not at regular intervals in a real letter box.

 What items would you keep in a letter box? Draw or stick them in.

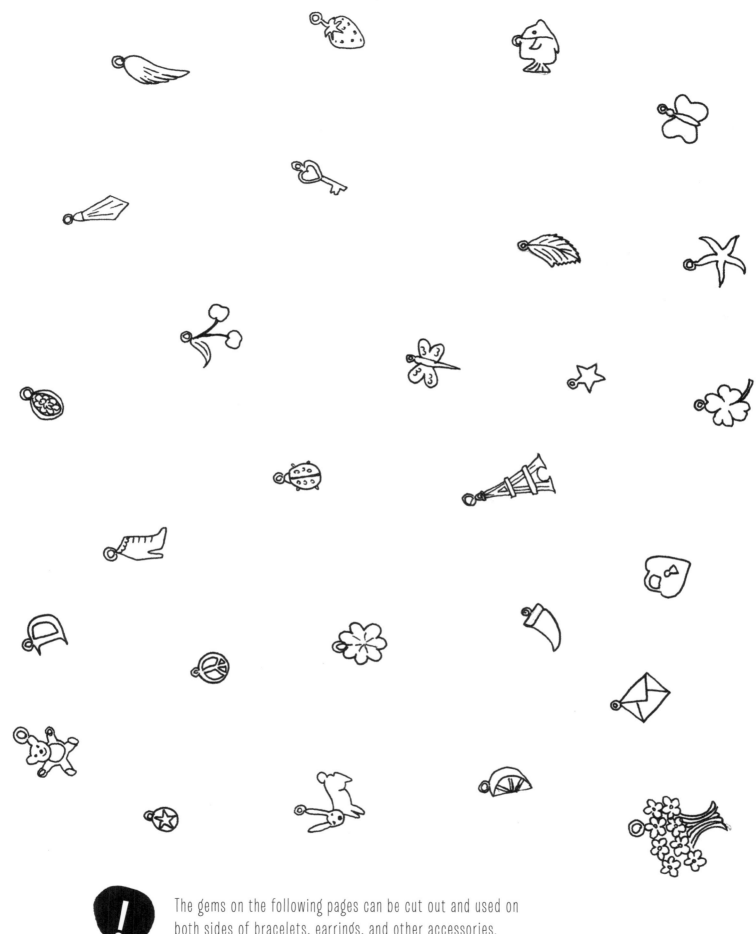

The gems on the following pages can be cut out and used on both sides of bracelets, earrings, and other accessories.

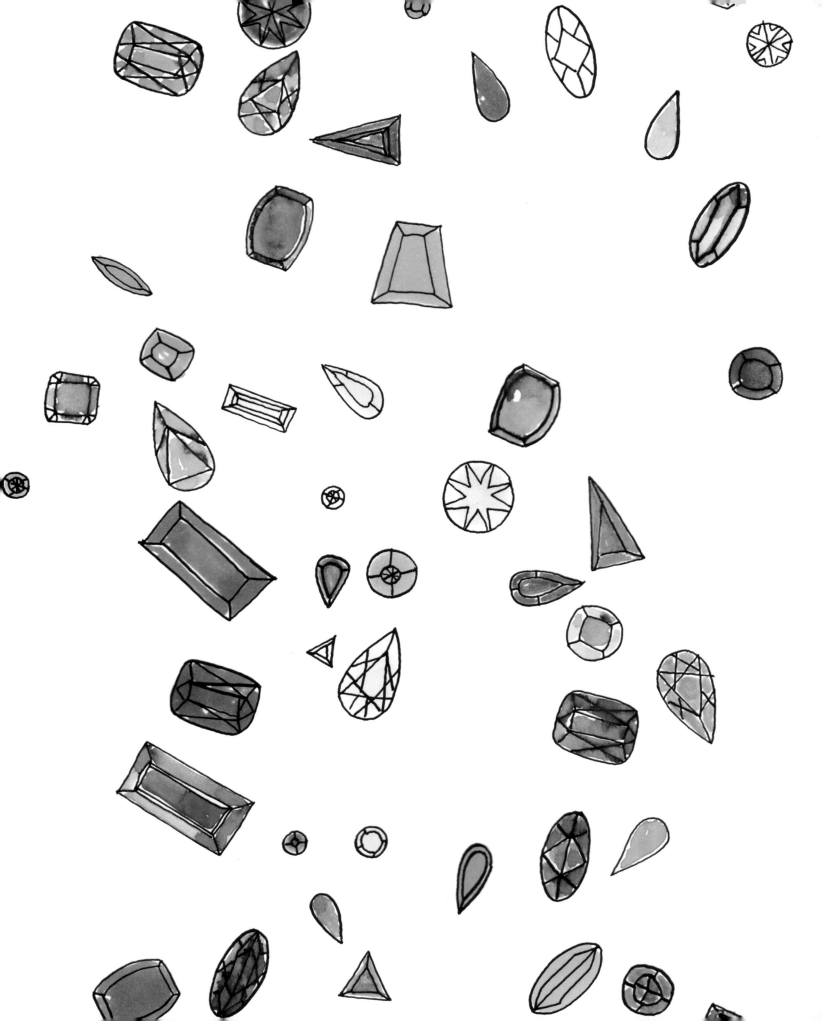

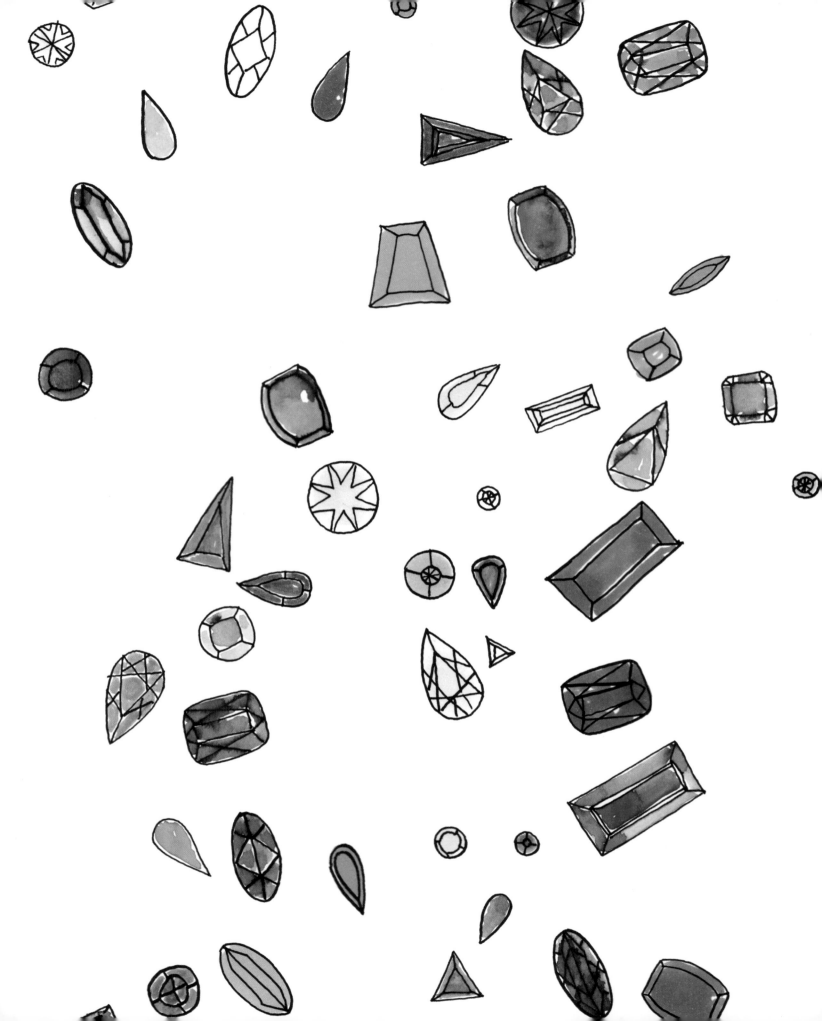

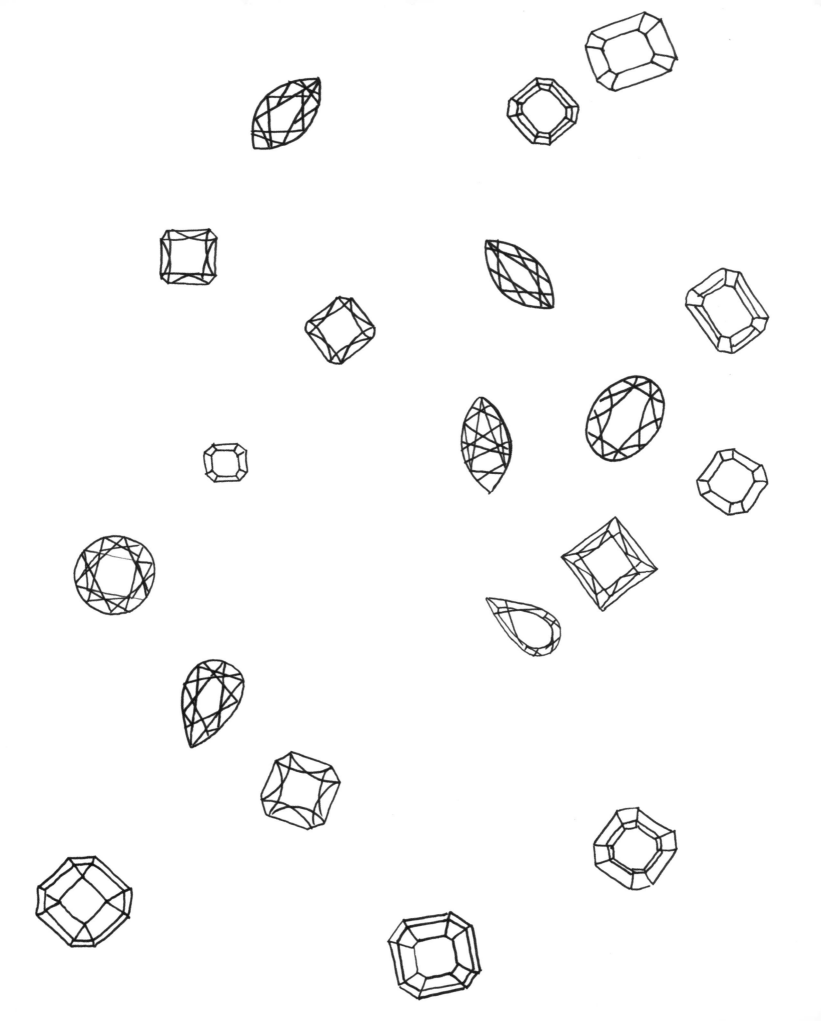

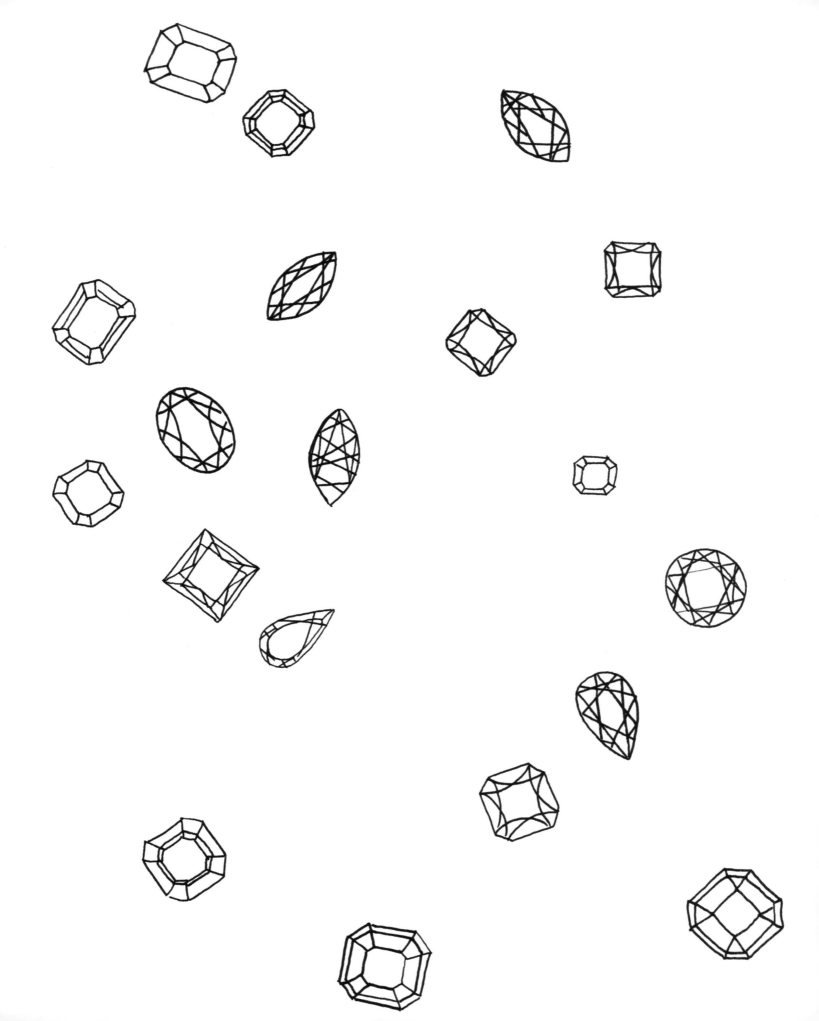

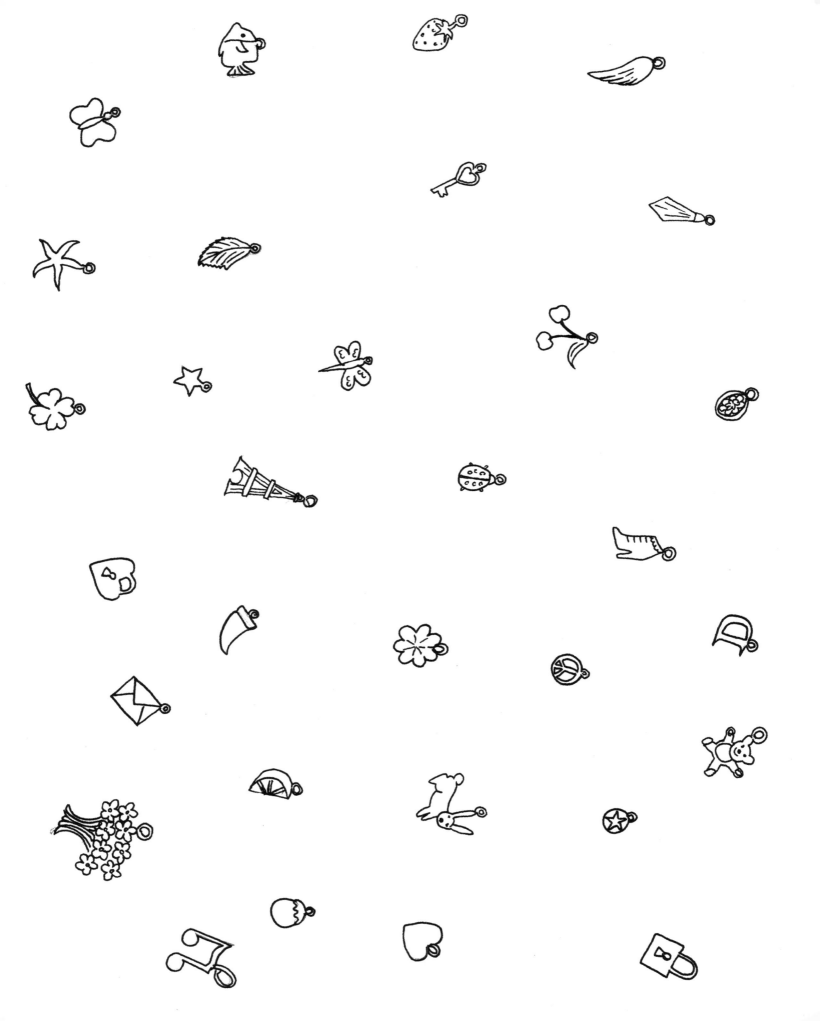

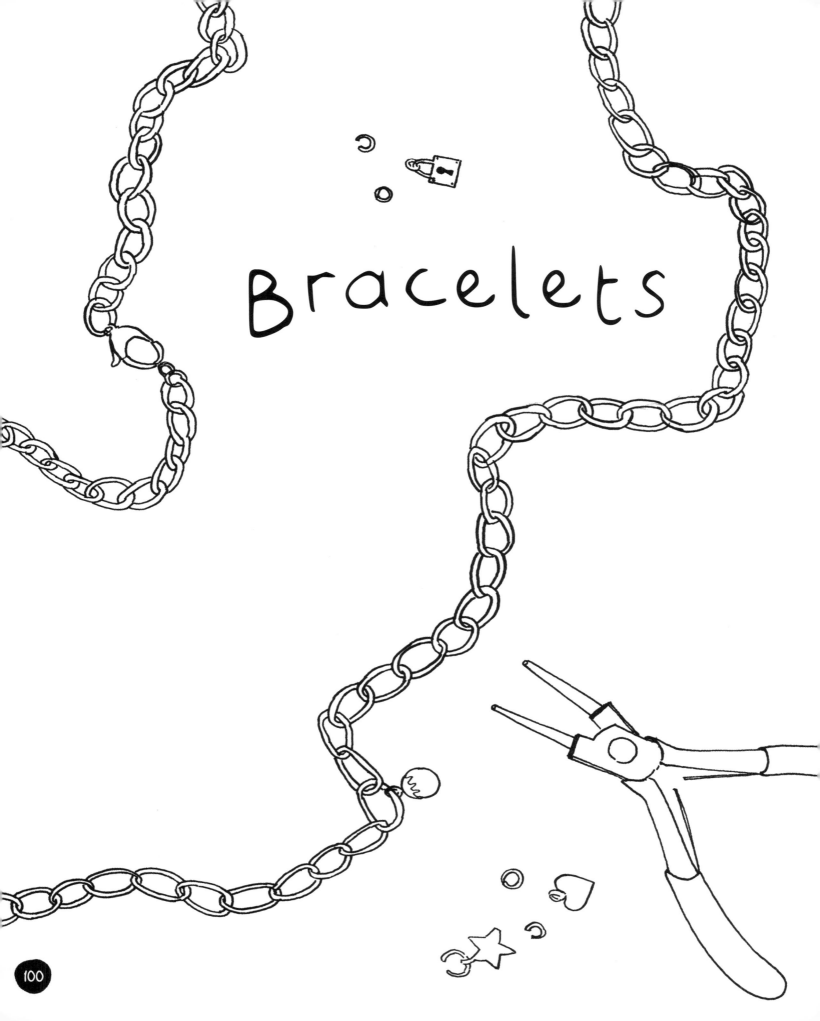

Bracelets

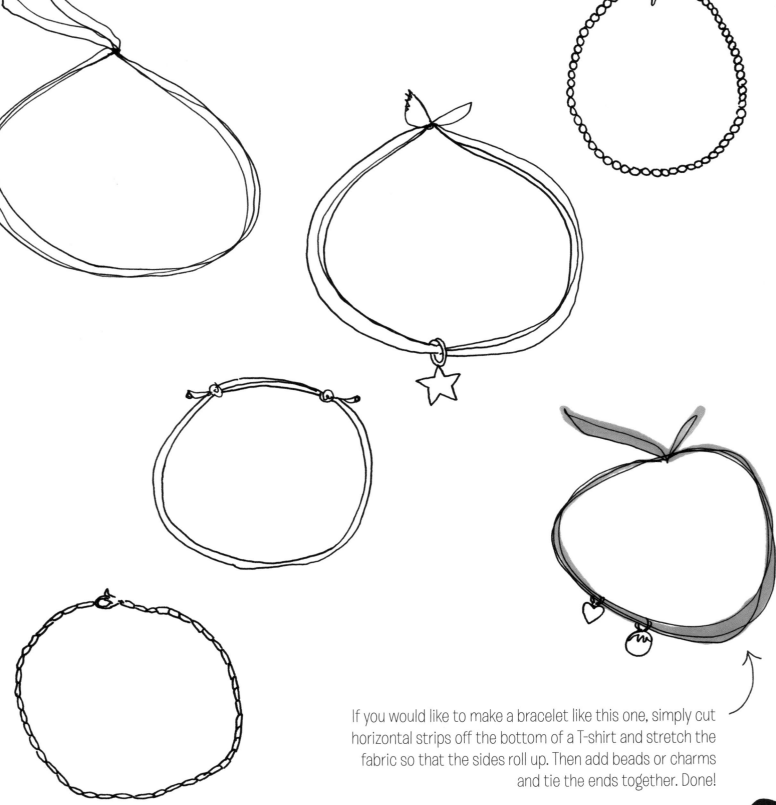

Use the charms and gems from the previous pages to decorate these bracelets.

If you would like to make a bracelet like this one, simply cut horizontal strips off the bottom of a T-shirt and stretch the fabric so that the sides roll up. Then add beads or charms and tie the ends together. Done!

The jewelry is missing on this page! Add rings, bracelets, or whatever other accessories you can think of.

Even nail polish can be used to add color.
Paint my nails for me or decorate this page.

My customers are looking for jewelry. What do you think would suit them?

Mismatch*?

*Mismatch : not matching

Not here!

 Combine patterns you don't think would match.
You'll probably find they go well together after all!

 Go crazy! Use all your favorite patterns and colors on these clothes and accessories.

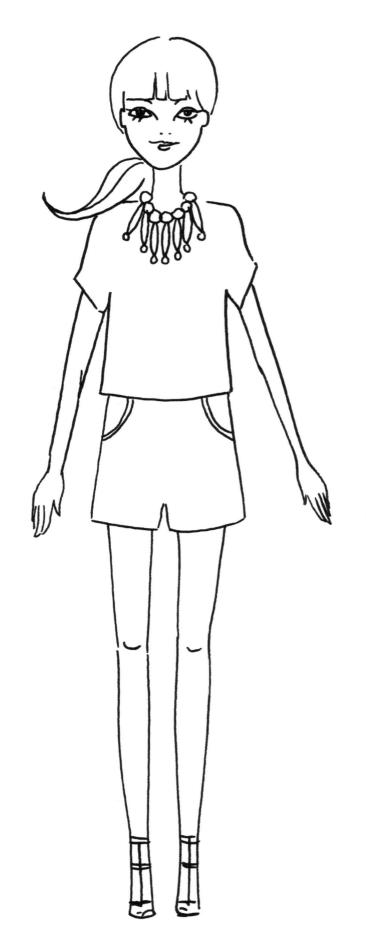

Wallpaper

 Design the background and my dress in the same pattern so I become invisible!

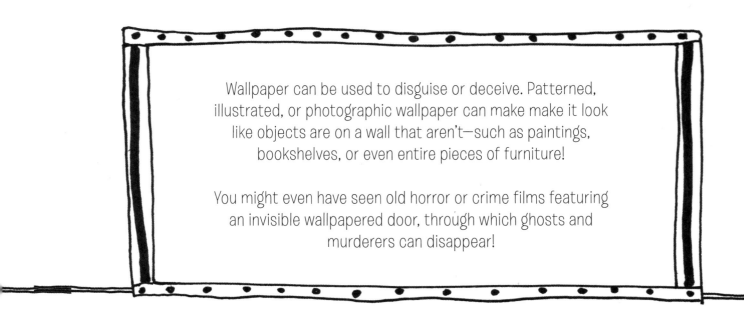

Wallpaper can be used to disguise or deceive. Patterned, illustrated, or photographic wallpaper can make make it look like objects are on a wall that aren't—such as paintings, bookshelves, or even entire pieces of furniture!

You might even have seen old horror or crime films featuring an invisible wallpapered door, through which ghosts and murderers can disappear!

Animal prints

My leopard print skirt suit is my favorite outfit to wear when I go bargain hunting.

Clothes, handbags, or shoes made of fur from tigers, hyenas, giraffes, or leopards were once a sign of wealth and exotic taste. This was especially true among bohemian people who lived in 1960s San Francisco and New York.

As many animal species around the world were in danger of extinction because of overhunting and illegal trade, the Endangered Species Act was passed in Washington in 1973. Since then, customs officials have been on the lookout for people returning from their travels with souvenirs made from endangered animals. These objects include elephant hooves as umbrella stands, jewelry made of feathers from rare birds, and tiger and zebra skins.

Many people didn't want to miss out on beautiful animal-skin patterns, however, so a new trend of animal prints sprang up in the fashion and textile industry.

Why not try it with some neon colors?

 Create your own animal print. Be inspired by cows, leopards, and giraffes . . .

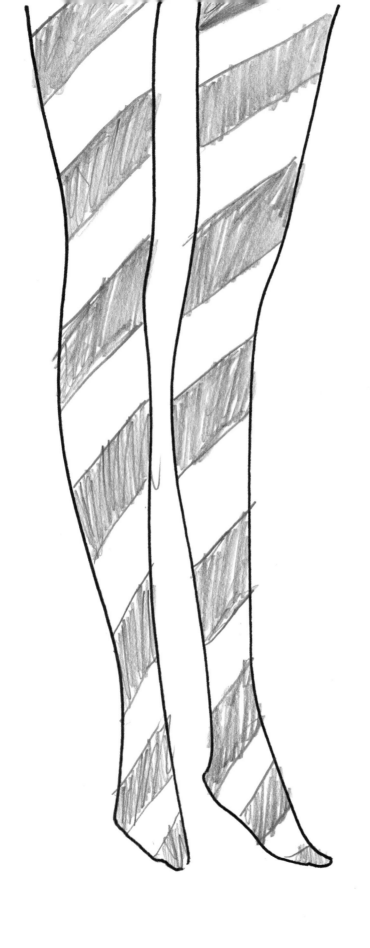

 Animal prints are great on tights . . .

Tights

I found this chic little black dress at a flea market in New York.

Have you seen tights with a black seam on the back? Draw them in here. Simple yet effective!

What's hiding behind these numbers?
Connect them and find out.

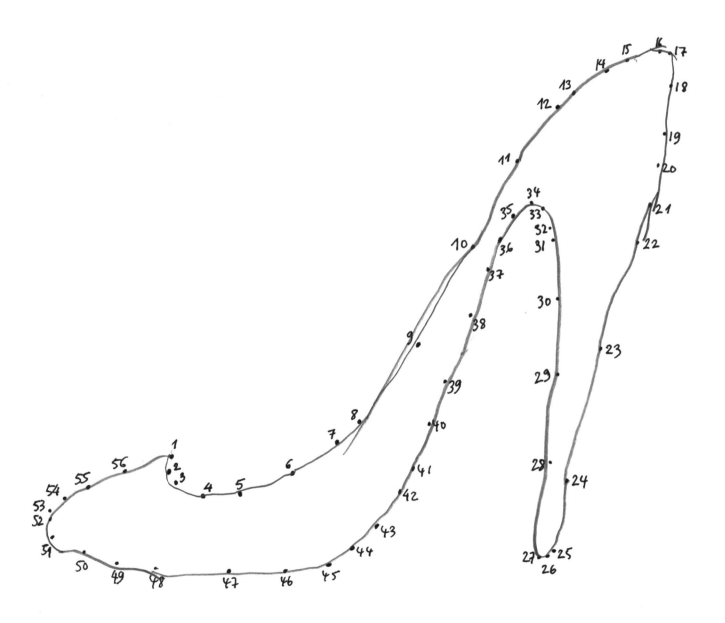

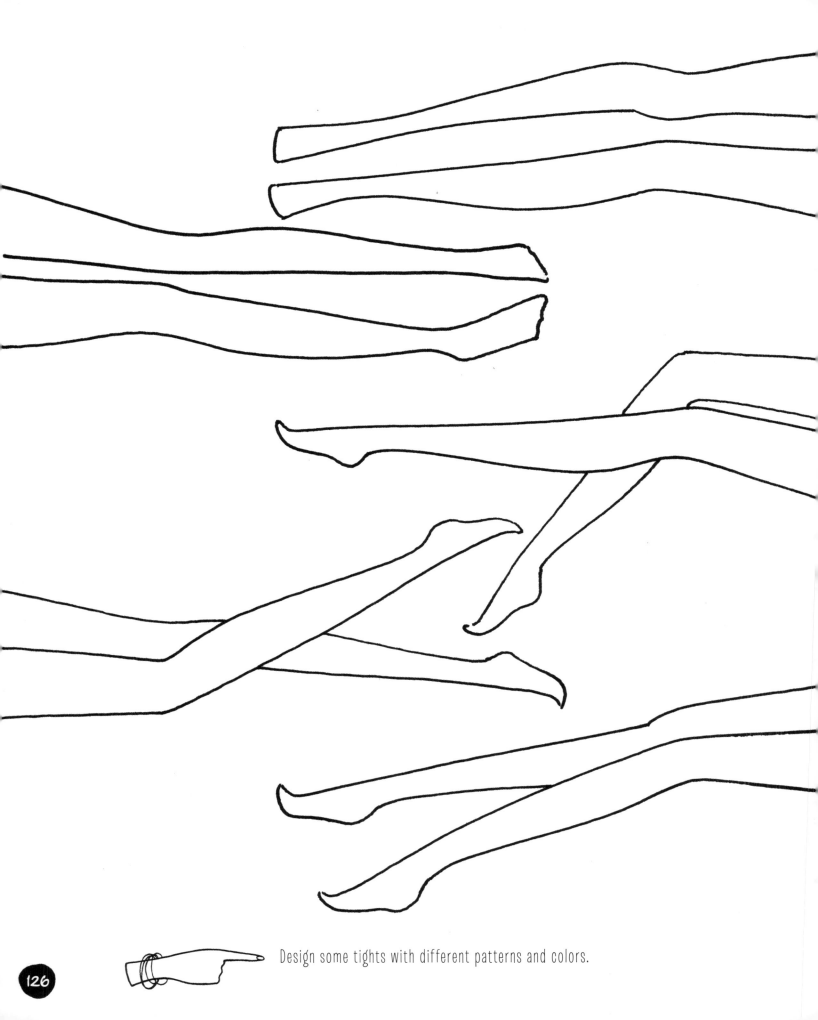

Design some tights with different patterns and colors.

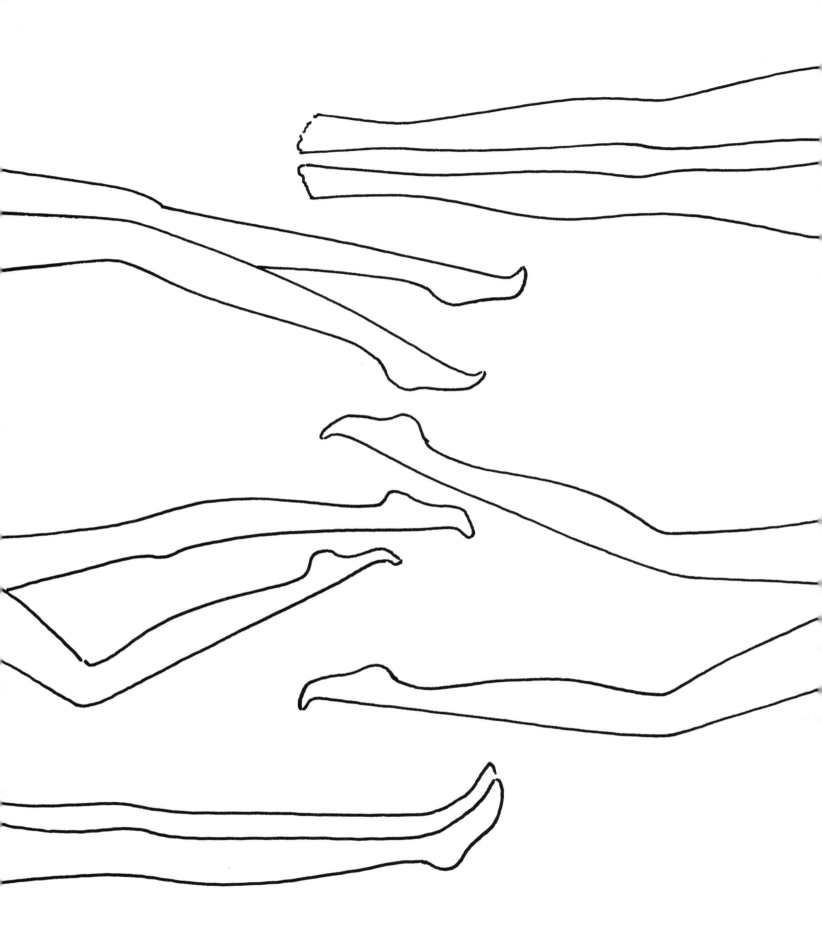

Decorate these bangles using gems. Check page 84 onwards for some examples.

Bakelite

The first industrially manufactured synthetic material was named after its inventor, Leo Baekeland. From 1909, Bakelite was used to make countless items from buttons to jewelry, and vacuums to radios. Production reached a peak in the 1930s, but Bakelite is not very impact resistant. Soon it was replaced by tougher materials. Nowadays Bakelite items are very popular among collectors because of their beautiful colors. I've often brought back Art-Deco brooches and necklaces from Paris. Today they are very rare and Bakelite is almost as expensive as gold.

Sunglasses

African scarf

Jewelry

Bakelite bangles

Jeans

Striped shirt

Knee-high socks
with polka dots

Here you can see the separate
items of Felicity's outfit. She's
a lovely regular customer of mine.
But what item is missing? Add it!

Handbag

Shoe
18th century

Let's go to the museum! Which items in your wardrobe are so old, unwearable, or precious that they are ready to go on display?

Fascinator

I made my own fascinator for my last spring ball. Chic, right? Maybe I should give courses in my shop.

Like many women's hat fashions, the fascinator originated in Britain. Many people outside the UK didn't know about this item before Prince William and Kate Middleton's wedding in 2011. Technically, the fascinator is not really a hat. It doesn't protect from sun or rain, but it is made of a combination of fabric, lace, feathers, and other materials. Sometimes a fascinator can look like a cloud, other times like a little figure. People who have no imagination whatsoever might refer to a particularly fancy or unusual creation as a "pretzel" or something equally unflattering!

 You can make your own fascinator by following these instructions. You won't need many materials, but it will look great!

YOU WILL NEED: one hairpin, strips of faux (artificial) leather, sequins, one or two feathers, sewing thread in a matching color, a cup, scissors, sewing needle, and PVA glue.

SEWING SEQUINS: The easiest way to sew sequins onto a strip of leather is to bring the needle up through the fabric where you want to place the sequin, and pull it onto the thread. Then go back into the fabric with your needle, as close to the edge of the sequin as possible. Pull the thread through and your first sequin is in place. Then come up through the fabric again, as close as possible to the first sequin, to sew on the next one. This way the sequins will overlap slightly. Just keep going the same way!

THIS IS HOW IT WORKS: Using a cup, draw two circles onto the back of the leather and cut them out. Then sew on the sequins, starting from the outside and circling inwards, ensuring that each row slightly overlaps the one before. Use different colors, or maybe even differently shaped sequins, for each row. Keep going until the circle is completely covered, then sew up the thread on the back in a few stitches.

FINISH: Add a little bit of PVA glue to the back of both circles. Lay the quills of the feathers between the center of both circles and then stick them together. This way all the stitches will be hidden. While the glue dries, stick the hairpin to the back of one of the circles. If the pin has holes you can also sew it onto the material. Once the glued-on hairpin has set (after a few hours, or preferably overnight) you're ready to show off your fascinator!

 Design fascinators made from foil or silk paper, for example. Create crazy shapes and stick them onto this page. Then decorate them using paint, feathers, or other materials.

 Using watercolors or acrylic paints, paint bold shapes onto this page.
Use the shapes to design fashionable fascinators.

Hats and shawls are great accessories. Design new patterns or cut out and glue on pictures of your favorite shawls. On the next page you can find a few examples of textile patterns. Be inspired!

Ikat fabric is not printed or painted. The pattern is made by dyeing single threads of material in the chosen colors before they are woven together. The shaky overlay pattern is typical of this method. Just like the tie-dye method, this approach is commonly used in Asia and for Indonesian sarongs, for example.

Ikat

 Draw the longest shawl in the world, or at least the second longest.

Label

Design your own label to adorn your designs. Use your initials or another combination of letters.

Dottie Polka

The idea of adding a manufacturer's permanent label to clothing can be traced back to fashion designer Paul Poiret. He was also one of the first designers to create women's clothing without a corset, so that the wearer could move more freely and comfortably.

I want to go out tonight. Will you help me choose a hairstyle?

Do you recognize these characters and people? Think of suitable outfits for their hairstyles, or create a contrasting design.

Geisha

Marie Antoinette

Princess Leia

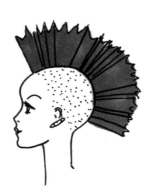

Punk mohawk

Twiggy

Jackie
Onassis

Time for some makeup. I wonder what suits me?
Use real eye shadow, powder and lip gloss—you'll
be surprised how the makeup behaves on paper!

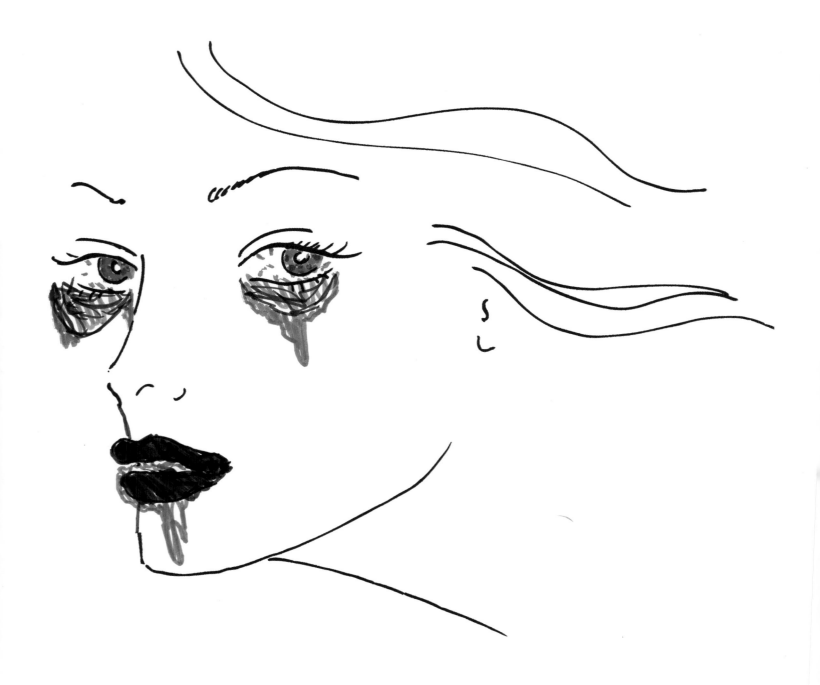

Eye shadow isn't just good for makeup: Karl Lagerfeld uses it to draw his designs. Try it! Color in these dresses with eye shadow and design your own outfit too (or two, or three . . .).

Chanel N°5

In the short-lived world of perfume, Chanel No. 5 is the longest-running designer scent, and it is still sold today. The scent and bottle are virtually unchanged since 1924. It's named after fashion designer Coco Chanel and her favorite number. It attained cult status after Marilyn Monroe's famous quote: "What do I wear in bed? Why, Chanel No. 5, of course."

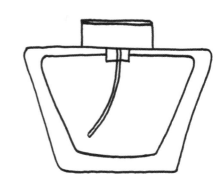

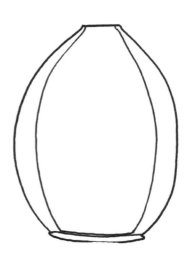

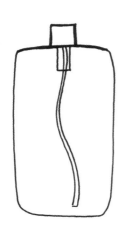

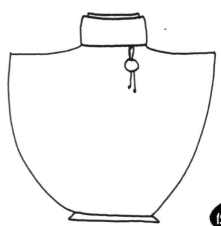

 What does the perfect perfume bottle look like in your opinion?
Design the missing bottle parts and think about differently
shaped perfume bottles for the tops.

 Blot this page with watercolors and other colored liquids and leave them to run.

 You can use polka dots to write too. Try it!

 These watches are missing their wristbands! Design various watchstraps. They don't all need to be made of leather!

 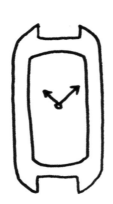 

Little black dress

The color black was traditionally reserved for funeral clothes. Yet when Coco Chanel declared that the "petit robe noir" would be the uniform of all women with good taste, the little black dress began its rise to fame.

It is often worn at special events like cocktail parties or formal functions, and was made particularly famous by Audrey Hepburn in *Breakfast at Tiffany's*. Her little black dress was designed by Givenchy.

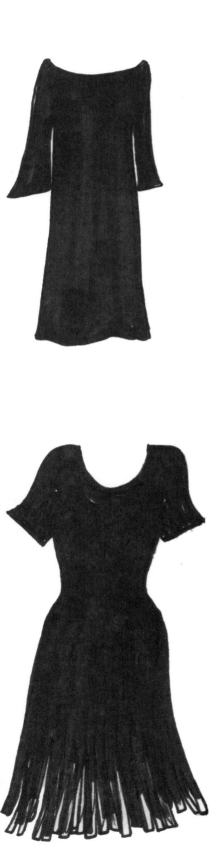

My favorite cocktail dress! I won it at an auction and loved it so much I simply couldn't sell it!

 Design your own "LBD." Think about what you can combine it with as well.
Find inspiration in fashion magazines or online fashion blogs.

 You can change a simple dress into something great with only a few materials. You can dye it, sew things onto it, add a collar, or cut tassels into it. Try it with these dresses!

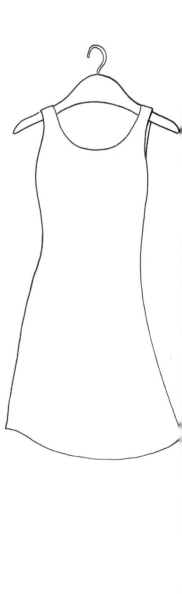

 If you fold over the next page you can have me try on different skirts.

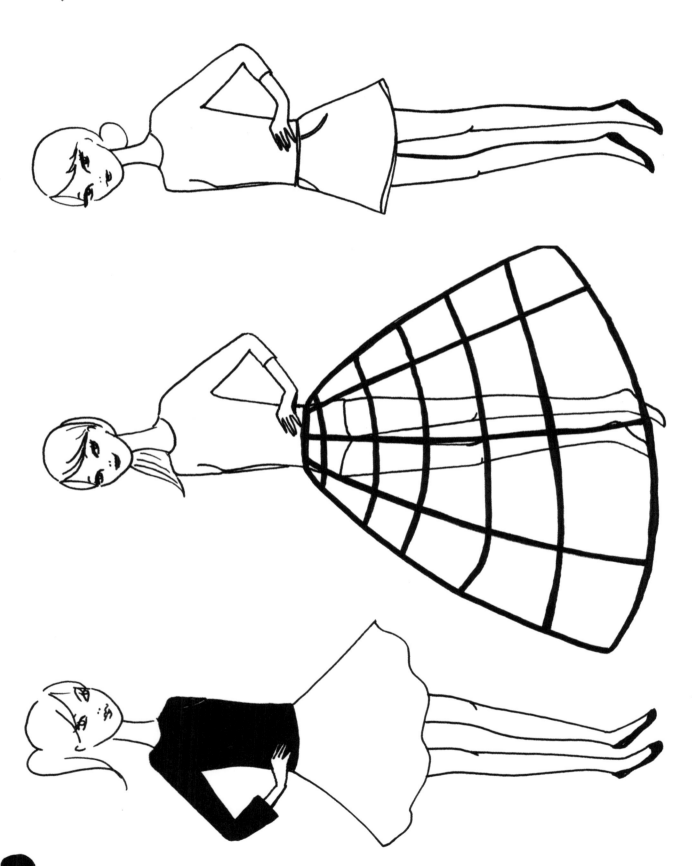

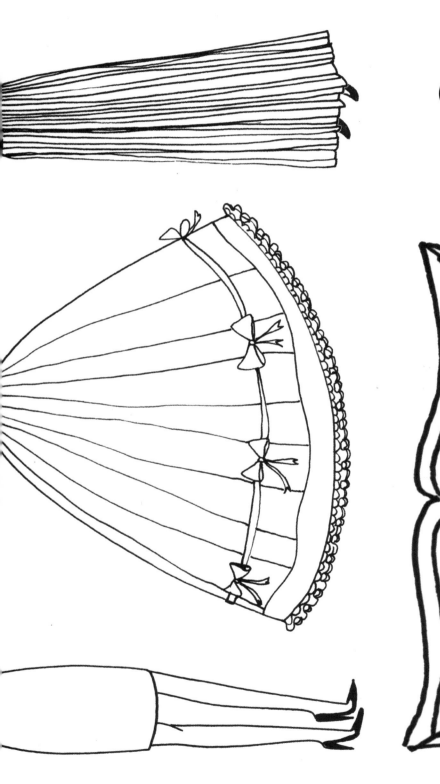

Crinoline

Have you ever seen women wearing huge skirts in films or paintings set in Victorian times? This type of skirt is called a crinoline. The whole thing is supported by a structure of steel. The circumference of the hem could measure up to twenty-six feet!

The crinoline had a brief revival in the 1950s when the bell-shaped petticoat was fashionable among teenagers. This model wasn't supported by a steel structure, but by being sprayed with potato starch.

 Draw a skirt made only of feathers!

 Decorate these skirts with patterns from the pattern book on page 179. Design your own models, too.

pattern book

When craftsmen showed work samples, door-to-door salesmen peddled their products, or dressmakers presented their fabrics, they would always use pattern books. These would contain a large variety of samples, but were easier to transport than the actual garments themselves. Whenever I find a rare pattern book, I always like to buy it. Books in which samples of fabric have been attached are especially precious.

 Be inspired by this dress made of snowflakes and design a dress made of flowers.

How long should this pleated skirt be? Shorten it to the length you want and decorate it with patterns.

Handbags

This is not a real Kelly bag, but I love its simple shape. I found it in a basement sale in New York.

What do you think I carry around in my handbag? Make a collage out of all the things you think my handbag should contain.

The Kelly bag is a famous handbag design by the French fashion house Hermès. It's been around since 1935 but didn't become famous until the American actress Grace Kelly wore it at her engagement to Monaco's Prince Rainier in 1956. Since then it has been known as the Kelly bag and is a symbol of royalty and good taste.

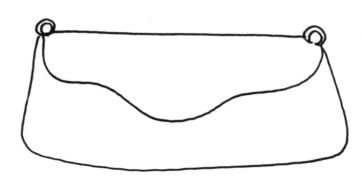

A handbag comes to life thanks to its handles or straps. Design the bags or handles that are missing. You can stick images from magazines onto this page, draw in your own, or use unusual materials.

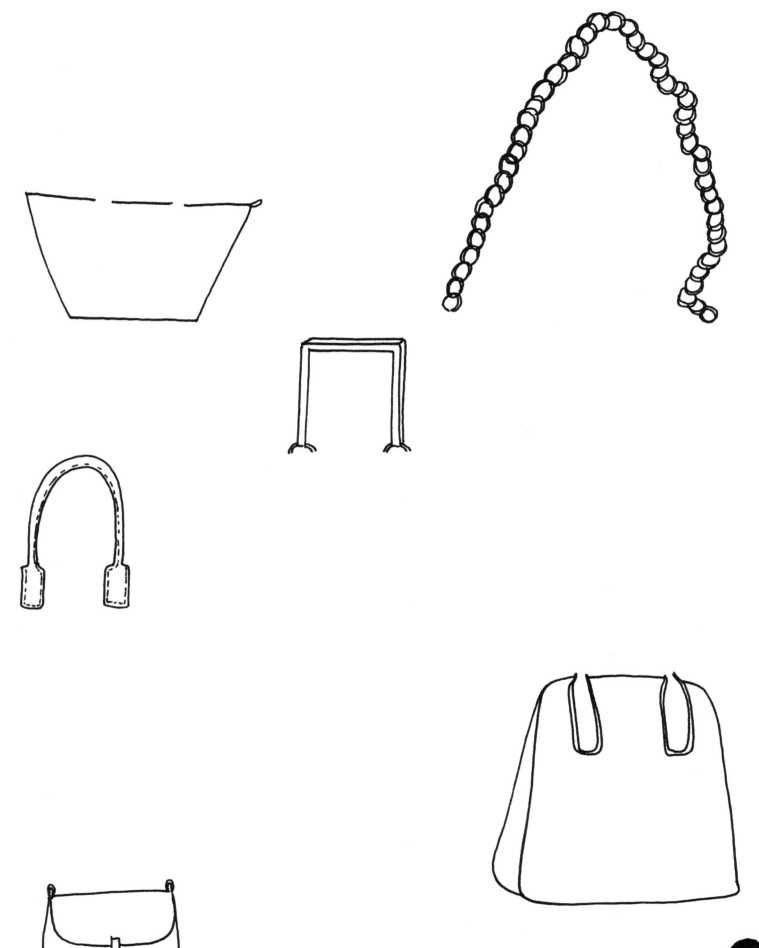

Bags like this one never stay in my shop for long. Everybody wants one!

 Use the stripes and see how you can create different effects, adding them horizontally and vertically. Maybe even diagonally or combine them.

191

Checked pattern

The Scottish tartan or checked pattern has become a bit unfashionable and is mostly found as lining in coats or as shawls. Nonetheless, entire generations of girls used to wear checked skirts. The checks are created by weaving together differently colored thread. Traditionally, different color combinations were used to symbolize the different families in Scotland. The tartans were not limited to textiles: You could buy printed tartan wrapping paper, as well as tartan plates, wooden containers, and boxes made of paper. Vicky squares are another classic pattern, most commonly in red and white, and often used in practical fashion. It's popular as shirt fabric for hikers and mountain climbers, and can also be found as table cloths and napkins in French bistros.

Swimwear

The pareo is a colorfully patterned piece of fabric that can be worn by women and men. It found its way onto the Mediterranean beaches of Europe from the island of Tahiti. The fabric, which is worn by skillfully wrapping it around the body, is tied in a clever way. The Indonesian sarong worn in Java and Bali is put on in a similar fashion.

 Fill in who is wearing these bathing suits and design your own or stick some onto this page. Then look for pareos in magazines and add your favorite using colored craft paper.

Everyone can wear a bikini, not just women who have the so-called "perfect bikini body." Choose a different body shape for each bikini and draw them in.

Bikini

When the first bikini appeared in 1946, it caused a scandal.
The two-piece bathing suit was banned for many years on beaches
in the Mediterranean and on the Atlantic coast. Even in Hollywood
films it was a no-no, until actresses such as Brigitte Bardot
helped to make the bikini more acceptable.

And then there was the hit song "Itsy Bitsy Teenie Weenie Yellow
Polka Dot Bikini" about a yellow two-piece with polka dots! When you
visit my shop I'll play the original record from 1960 for you!

Burkini

For girls in Muslim countries it's still difficult to find appropriate things to wear to go swimming. In the past they wouldn't go swimming at all, or did so fully dressed in their normal clothes. The designer Aheda Zanetti solved this dilemma by inventing the burkini, a pajama-like outfit made from synthetic fiber.

 My friend Serap found a burkini in my shop. She still wants to make it look a bit prettier. How would you do that?

Which 18 items of clothing and accessories could you
not live without? Record them on this page.

Collections

Fall/Winter

The wheel of fashion turns faster and faster. The seasons are still the main drivers, so there are collections for Fall/Winter as well as Spring/Summer. Because the collections follow one another so quickly, designers, manufacturers, and distributors are under immense pressure. A knitwear company will wait until the very last minute to dye its products, for example, in order to ensure that they hit the correct color for that fashion season.

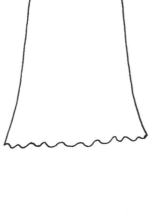

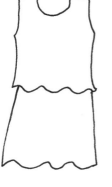

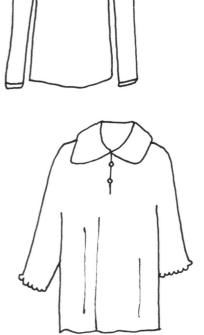

Design the clothes on this double page as a Fall/Winter collection, then on the next page as Spring/Summer. Use the latest color trends or simply create your very own collection.

spring/summer

 Are you ready for the final show? Reveal
your best creations on the runway!
Who should sit in the front row at your
fashion show? Put together a wish list
of your audience.

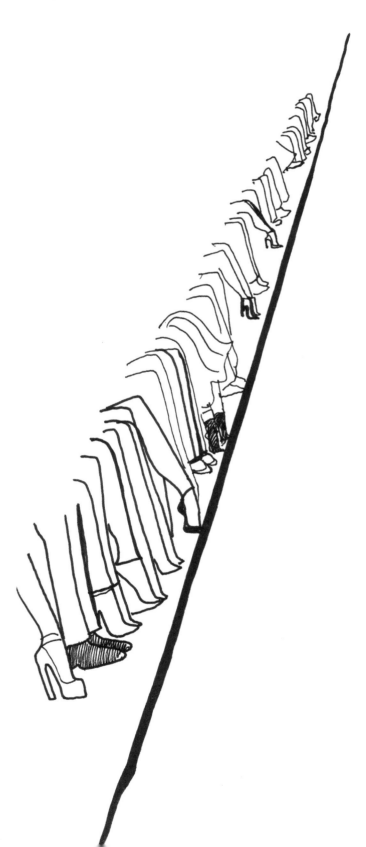

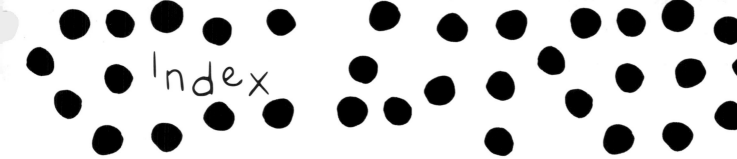

Index

little bee books

An imprint of Bonnier Publishing Group
853 Broadway, New York, New York 10003

Copyright © 2013 by Edition Michael Fischer GmbH. This little bee books edition, 2015.
All rights reserved, including the right of reproduction in whole or in part in any form.
LITTLE BEE BOOKS is a trademark of Bonnier Publishing Group, and associated colophon is a
trademark of Bonnier Publishing Group.

Manufactured in China 0231214

First Edition 2 4 6 8 10 9 7 5 3 1

ISBN 978-1-4998-0031-9

www.littlebeebooks.com

www.bonnierpublishing.com

Dottie Polka.